The Essential Reading and Language Arts Glossary III

A Student Reference Guide

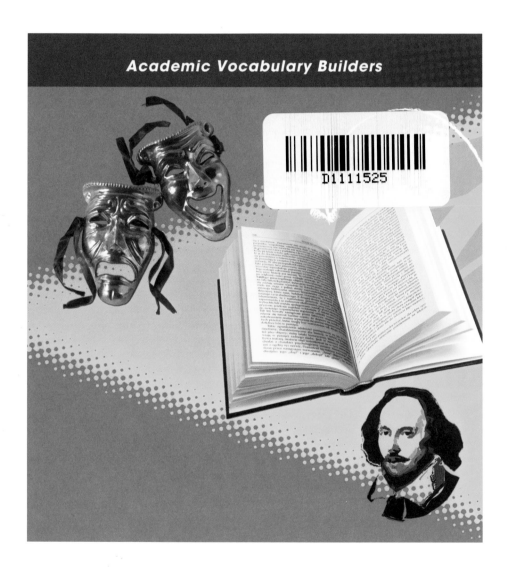

Academic Vocabulary Builders

D1111525

red brick
LEARNING

Academic Vocabulary Builders are published by Red Brick Learning
7825 Telegraph Road, Bloomington, Minnesota 55438
http://www.redbricklearning.com

Library of Congress Cataloging-in-Publication Data
The essential reading and language arts glossary III : a student reference guide.
    p. cm. — (Academic vocabulary builders)
    Includes index.
    ISBN-13: 978-1-4296-2725-2 (hardcover)
    ISBN-10: 1-4296-2725-5 (hardcover)
    1. Vocabulary — Study and teaching (Elementary) 2. Vocabulary — Juvenile literature.
3. Reading (Elementary). 4. Language arts (Elementary). I. Title: Essential reading and
language arts glossary 3. II. Series.
LB1574.5.E874 2009
372.44 — dc22   2008021906

Cover design
Ted Williams

Design and Illustration:
Sasha Blanton
SGB Design Solutions

1 2 3 4 5 6 13 12 11 10 09 08

Table of Contents

About this book:

This book will help you learn essential words you will need to understand to do well on state tests. These essential words will also help you to do well in school.

There are almost 230 Reading and Language Arts words and definitions in the book. They are listed in alphabetical order under six main topics.

Here is a sample word with its features:

Easy to read definitions

Autobiography

A book that someone writes about his or her own life.

The former slave Booker T. Washington wrote a book about his own life. His **autobiography** is called *Up From Slavery*.

Pictures to help understanding   Examples in context

Reading Strategies

READING
STRATEGIES

LITERARY
CONCEPTS

WRITING

LANGUAGE
CONVENTIONS

RESEARCH

PRINTING
&
PUBLISHING

Analysis

A conclusion that you make by using a combination of new information and what you already know.

Careful **analysis** of a baseball game can help you learn to be a better baseball player.

Antonym

A word that has the opposite meaning of another word.

The **antonym** of *big* is *small*.

Compare

To look at two or more things and find ways in which they are the same.

I **compared** apples and oranges. I found that they are both sweet fruits.

Connotation

The secondary meaning of a word. This meaning includes how a word makes you feel.

The words *house* and *home* may have the same meaning in the dictionary, but *home* seems to have a second meaning that is warmer and happier than the word *house*. *House* has a neutral **connotation**, while *home* has a warm, positive **connotation**.

1

Context

The words and ideas surrounding a word or phrase in a passage that can help you figure out its meaning.

After I took one bite of *wasabi*, I felt like my mouth was on fire.

In this sentence, the **context** words *bite* and *on fire* help you know that *wasabi* is most likely a very spicy food, even if you have never seen the word *wasabi* before.

Contrast

To look at two or more things and find ways in which they are different.

I **contrasted** apples and oranges. They are different colors. Apples have smooth skin. Oranges have rough skin.

Denotation

The meaning of a word as it would appear in a dictionary.

The words *house* and *home* have the same **denotation**. They both mean "a place where people live."

Details

Information that tells about the main idea of a paragraph or gives a lot of information about one specific thing.

Details of a tree:
Tall trunk
Bumpy bark
Green leaves

Reading Strategies

Dialect

The words or phrases used by people from a certain place or background.

"What can I get y'all?" asked the waitress in a thick Texas **dialect**.

Evidence

Information that will help you prove your ideas in an essay or other piece of writing. **Evidence** is sometimes called *proof*.

Anna wanted to prove that plants grow better when they are in the sun. She used **evidence** from her science book that said, "Plants need sunlight to live."

Expository writing

Writing that tells facts or explains things. Writing that is **expository** does not try to present a person's opinion.

A driver's manual is an example of **expository writing**.

Graphic organizer

A chart that helps you put your ideas in order so that you can better understand them.

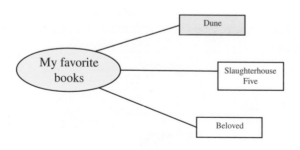

READING STRATEGIES

LITERARY CONCEPTS

WRITING

LANGUAGE CONVENTIONS

RESEARCH

PRINTING & PUBLISHING

READING STRATEGIES

LITERARY CONCEPTS

WRITING

LANGUAGE CONVENTIONS

RESEARCH

PRINTING & PUBLISHING

Highlight

To make a word or phrase stand out so it is easier to find within a text or passage. If you **highlight** important words when you first write them down, it will be easier to find them when you study your notes later.

The Amazon River is the second largest river in the world.

Main idea

The most important point in a piece of writing.

In a news article about trees, the **main idea** of the article might be, "Trees are good for the environment."

Media

A means to communicate or send messages. Some examples are: television, radio, newspapers, and magazines.

TV, radio, newspapers, and magazines are all types of **media**.

The word **media** is plural. The singular form of **media** is *medium*.
TV is a **medium**.
TV, radio, and newspapers are **media**.

Reading Strategies

Narrative

A story or event that is written down or spoken out loud. A **narrative** is often more descriptive than simple reporting.

> **Reporting**

Yesterday, two women were shopping for apples at the local market. They were planning to make an apple pie for their mother.

> **Narrative**

It was the day before Mom's birthday, and Jean and Tess had big plans. Looking at apples as if they were red jewels, Jean said, "This is going to be the best apple pie ever!"

Notes

The words and phrases you write down as you listen to your teacher or read a passage. **Notes** are written in a notebook to help you remember the most important parts of a lesson or a piece of writing.

LITERARY
CONCEPTS

WRITING

LANGUAGE
CONVENTIONS

RESEARCH

PRINTING
&
PUBLISHING

① *Pronouns*
  replace a noun
  save space
  don't have to keep repeating a name
  I, you, he, she, it, etc.
② *Proper nouns*
  tell that something is important
  usually names of people or places
  Uncle John, Paris, the Waldorf Mall

READING STRATEGIES

LITERARY CONCEPTS

WRITING

LANGUAGE CONVENTIONS

RESEARCH

PRINTING & PUBLISHING

Problem

The part of a story that needs to be solved.

Dani heads home after a long day at school. She pushes open the front door, throws her backpack on the floor, and heads toward the kitchen for a snack. And then it hits her: *Something is missing here. Where's Sparky? He always jumps up on me as soon as I get home. He needs to be walked! Where is my dog?*

In this story, the **problem** is: *How do you find the missing dog?*

Proof

Information that shows that something is true. **Proof** is sometimes called *evidence*.

It is important to do well in school.
Proof: Studies show that people who do well in school are more likely to find good jobs or go to college.

Propaganda

Ideas spread on purpose to convince people to act in a certain way or believe as others do.

During World War II, many countries used **propaganda** to keep their people in good spirits as bad things continued to happen.

Solution

An answer, or the way to fix a problem.

Dani heads home after a long day at school. She pushes open the front door, throws her backpack on the floor, and heads toward the kitchen for a snack. And then it hits her: *Something is missing here. Where's Sparky? He always jumps up on me as soon as I get home. He needs to be walked! Where is my dog?*

In this story, the **solution** is that Dani and her dad make "Lost Dog" signs and post them all over the town.

Summary

A short statement of the most important ideas or events in a passage or story.

Summary of the *Wizard Of Oz***:**
Dorothy's house was picked up by a tornado and dropped in a magical land. She wanted to get back to her home and family. She found some shoes that a mean witch wanted to have. She made friends as she tried to find her way back home. These friends helped her stop the mean witch from taking her shoes. Finally, the shoes, which were magical, helped her get back home.

Synonym

A word that has the same or close to the same meaning as another word.

A **synonym** for *large* is *big*.

Time Line

A graphic organizer that shows events from a story in the order they happened.

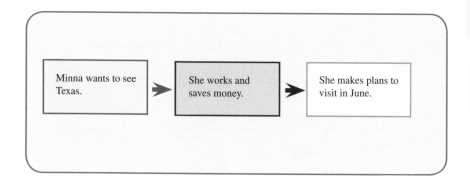

Venn diagram

A graphic organizer that uses overlapping circles to show how two items are similar and different.

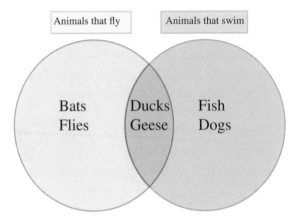

Visual aid

A picture, illustration, or graphic organizer that helps you understand an idea.

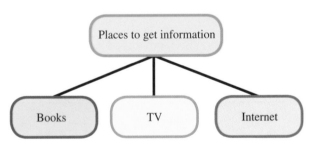

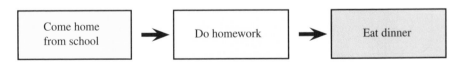

Literary Concepts

Allegory

A story in which the characters or events are symbols of ideas.

In the **allegory** of the "Turtle and the Rabbit," the turtle represents patience and finishing what you start. The rabbit represents speed and not taking the time to do a job well.

Alliteration

Repeating consonant or vowel sounds at the beginning of words.

Pat **p**icked **p**eppers for his **p**izza.

Analogy

A relationship between two sets of words, stories, or ideas.

Analogy can also be found in tests, in a very specific format using *like* or *as*.

Birds are to *sky* as *fish* are to *water*.

Anecdote

A short story of a minor event which is told to entertain.

For my little sister's birthday, I wanted to give her a dollhouse for her favorite doll. I spent all month saving up my money for that dollhouse. When her birthday finally came, just as I was about to give her the present, my sister said to the whole family, "I'm too big for dolls now. For my birthday, all I want is a bike!"

READING STRATEGIES

LITERARY CONCEPTS

WRITING

LANGUAGE CONVENTIONS

RESEARCH

PRINTING & PUBLISHING

Literary Concepts

READING STRATEGIES

LITERARY CONCEPTS

WRITING

LANGUAGE CONVENTIONS

RESEARCH

PRINTING & PUBLISHING

Anthropomorphism

Giving human characteristics to gods, animals, or things.

In the story *Alice in Wonderland*, the White Rabbit is an **anthropomorphic** character who talks to Alice just like a human.

Assonance

Repeated vowel sounds in a series of words. The vowel sounds can be anywhere in the word, not just at the beginning.

We appr*o*ached the *o*ld g*o*at on the st*o*ny r*o*ad.

Audience

The people who will read, see, or hear anything that is written, spoken, or presented. This word usually means a group of people in one place, such as a movie theater. In the case of a book's **audience**, it means every person who has read the book.

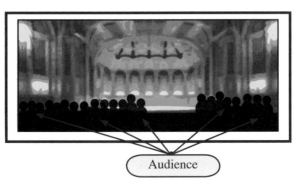

Audience

Autobiography

A book that someone writes about his or her own life.

The former slave Booker T. Washington wrote a book about his own life. His **autobiography** is called *Up From Slavery*.

Literary Concepts

Biography
A book that someone writes about someone else's life.

Dale read a **biography** about George Washington, the first president of the United States.

Character
A person in a story, play, or movie.

*Main **character***:

In the *Wizard of Oz*, Dorothy is the main **character**.

*Supporting **character***:

In the *Wizard of Oz*, the Scarecrow, Tin Man and Lion are supporting **characters**.

Characterization
The way an author describes the looks, actions, and thoughts of a character along with how others think about that character.

The **characterization** of Atticas Finch in *To Kill a Mockingbird* is that of a good, honest man. As a father, he tries to raise his two children to treat others fairly. The people in his town turn to him for advice and help.

Climax

The high point of a story. This happens when the conflict reaches a turning point.

In a story about a missing dog, the **climax** would be when one of the characters says, "I found the dog!"

Comedy

A type of story in which things turn out well for the main characters. **Comedies** are often funny.

Conflict

The struggle between two or more forces or characters in a story.

Conflict can be between people who might want to own the same buried treasure. **Conflict** can also be between a character and an animal or between a character and the weather.

Couplet

In a poem, two lines with the same meter that rhyme at the end. These are often found at the end of sonnets

The pretty flowers and birds that sing
Are clues to let you know it's Spring.

Dialogue

The words that characters say to each other. In writing, **dialogue** is usually shown in quotation marks.

"Where do you want to go?" asked Louis.
"Let's go to the park!" said Darnell.

Direct quote

A statement, usually written, of exactly what someone has said. **Direct quotes** are written in quotation marks.

President Abraham Lincoln once said, **"A house divided against itself cannot stand."**

Documentary

A movie that shows the facts about a subject.

In science class, we watched a **documentary** about birds. It showed us many different kinds of birds, what they eat, and how they sing.

READING STRATEGIES

LITERARY CONCEPTS

WRITING

LANGUAGE CONVENTIONS

RESEARCH

PRINTING & PUBLISHING

Literary Concepts

READING
STRATEGIES

**LITERARY
CONCEPTS**

WRITING

LANGUAGE
CONVENTIONS

RESEARCH

PRINTING
&
PUBLISHING

Drama

Another word for a *play*. People often use the word **drama** when they are talking about a serious play.

Romeo and Juliet is an example of a **drama**.

Epic

A long narrative poem about a famous hero or heroine.

The Odyssey is an **epic** about a man who goes off to war for many years.

Fiction

A narrative that is not true.

Fairy tales are **fiction** because they could not happen in real life. Realistic **fiction** sounds like real life but is actually about made-up characters.

Alice in Wonderland and *Oliver Twist* are both examples of **fiction**.

Figure of speech

A string of words that is used to mean something other than its true, or *literal*, meaning. Figures of speech make writing seem more expressive.

Her mind was **on fire with ideas**.

This sentence does not *literally* mean the girl's mind is on fire. The sentence uses the **figure of speech** "on fire with ideas" to show that the girl was coming up with many exciting and creative ideas at once.

Literary Concepts

Flashback

A sudden jump back in time to an earlier event in a story or movie.

Many **flashbacks** in books and movies show you a character's childhood. **Flashbacks** help you better understand a character.

Foreshadow

To give clues at the beginning of a story that hint at what will happen later.

If a character talks about how much he loves to ride bicycles with friends, this might be a clue. It may **foreshadow** a bicycle race that will happen later.

Genre

The type or kind of a piece of writing.

The most popular **genres** are fiction, poetry, and plays.

Historical narrative

A story set during a specific time in history. The story can be fiction or nonfiction.

Reading a **historical narrative** is a fun way to learn about history.

Thoth

READING STRATEGIES

LITERARY CONCEPTS

WRITING

LANGUAGE CONVENTIONS

RESEARCH

PRINTING & PUBLISHING

Literary Concepts

Imagery

Words that help you see, feel, or hear things in a passage.

In autumn, the leaves bake slowly into yellows and oranges, and a crisp, smoky smell rides on the breeze.

In this example, the words *bake, yellow*, *crisp* and *smoky* are **imagery** that help you imagine the scene.

Lyric poem

A **poem** that usually tells about the writer's feelings on some topic.

Excerpt from Robert Frost's *Stopping By Woods On A Snowy Evening*

Whose woods these are I think I know.
His house is in the village though;
He will not see me stopping here
To watch his woods fill up with snow.

In this **lyric poem**, the writer cares deeply about the snowy weather and quiet woods.

Metaphor

A figure of speech that describes one thing as being the same as another thing.

He had a **heart of stone**.

In this sentence, the person does not really have a heart made out of stone. The **metaphor** *heart of stone* is a way to compare someone who is not loving to a hard, cold stone.

Literary Concepts

Monologue

A part of a play where one character talks for a long time about one topic without being interrupted. Often during a **monologue**, the character is alone on stage.

Shakespeare used **monologues** in many of his works.

Mood

The feeling a story creates for the reader.

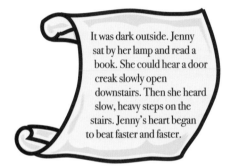

It was dark outside. Jenny sat by her lamp and read a book. She could hear a door creak slowly open downstairs. Then she heard slow, heavy steps on the stairs. Jenny's heart began to beat faster and faster.

Myth

A story that tells about the lives of gods, goddesses, and other heroes. Often, **myths** explain things in the world like sunrises, floods, or hurricanes.

The ancient Greeks explained sunrises and sunsets with the **myth** of the god Helios, who drives the sun across the sky every day.

Narrative poem

A **poem** that tells a story.

Beowulf is a very old **narrative poem** about a brave man who fights a giant monster.

Narrator

A person who tells a story.

Nonfiction

Writing that is based on facts.

 Newspapers tell about real people and events, so they are **nonfiction**.

Novel

A long, fictional story.

War and Peace is a classic **novel**.

Oxymoron

A figure of speech that is made of two opposite words or ideas. When put together, the two words or ideas make sense.

The ice was **burning cold**.
For dinner, we had **jumbo shrimp**.

Personal narrative

An autobiography that is written by someone who is not well-known.

Your diary is an example of a **personal narrative**.

Personification

A description of things or ideas as if they were human.

Winter is often described as *angry* and *cruel*. These are human qualities that can make winter seem like a person or character. Winter has the **personification** of an angry, cruel person.

Play

A story that is acted out on a stage. (also see *drama*)

READING
STRATEGIES

LITERARY
CONCEPTS

WRITING

LANGUAGE
CONVENTIONS

RESEARCH

PRINTING
&
PUBLISHING

READING STRATEGIES

LITERARY CONCEPTS

WRITING

LANGUAGE CONVENTIONS

RESEARCH

PRINTING & PUBLISHING

Plot

A series of events in a story or play.

An example of a simple **plot**:
Two people meet by accident, talk, and become friends.

Poem

Lines of words that either tell a story or tell about an emotion.
They are written in a special form, such as sonnets or ballads, and
sometimes rhyme.

> The rain is falling all around,
> It falls on field and tree,
> It rains on the umbrellas here,
> And on the ships at sea.
> -R. L. Stevenson

Poetry

Writing that is in a patterned form of lines using meter, rhythm,
and rhyme. **Poetry** is also defined as *writing that is not prose*.

Prose	**Poetry**
Today was the first day of school. I had a great time during the summer. Now I'm ready to start learning!	Walking back to school, Past the shops and past the park. No more summers in the pool; I'll be learning 'til it's dark.

Literary Concepts

Point of view

The person or character from whose eyes we see a story.

First-person **point of view** (the **me** point of view):
I'm in tenth grade at Jamestown High School. It's been a great day, and it's only the first day back to school.

Third-person **point of view** (the **he** or **she** point of view):
Derek is in tenth grade at Jamestown High School. He's had a great day, and it's only his first day back to school.

Prose

Any form of writing that sounds like normal speech and does not have obvious meter and rhyme. **Prose** is also defined as *writing that is not poetry*.

Prose	**Poetry**
Today was the first day of school. I had a great time during the summer. Now I'm ready to start learning!	Walking back to school, Past the shops and past the park. No more summers in the pool; I'll be learning 'til it's dark.

Resolution

The events that lead the characters to a settled state after the climax of the story. This is when the conflict has been solved.

In a story about a missing dog, the **resolution** would begin when the dog is found. The **resolution** might include bringing the dog back home and giving it extra dog treats.

Rhyme

To have the same end sounds.

bake, cake, flake
fly, sky, pie

Rhythm

A pattern of stressed sounds in writing. This is often seen in poetry.

Once up**on** a **mid**night **drear**y, **while** I **pon**dered

weak and **wear**y…

Satire

A story that makes fun of people's actions or mistakes.

Setting

The place and time that a story happens.

The **setting** of *The Great Gatsby* is Long Island, New York, in the mid-1920s.

Short story

A story that can be read at one sitting.

The Tell-Tale Heart is a famous short story. It is only a few pages long.

Simile

A comparison of two things using *like* or *as*.

Her hair is soft *like* silk.

Sonnet

A poem that has exactly 14 lines. The lines are put together in a specific form and sometimes end in a couplet.

Spring Is Here

With crisp green blades of grass between your toes,
And chirping birdsong flowing to your ear;
With sweet refreshing air inside your nose,
The long-awaited clues that Spring is here.
Forget about the long cold months of snow,
The ice-packed streets, the ever-present chill.
It's out into the glorious Sun you go!
And of the warming sunshine get your fill.
To beaches, lakes, or parks for picnic-time
Then laze about and snooze away the day
Or read a book, so up a tree you climb
Soft rays illuminating where you lay
Soon Spring slides into Summer, heat and all
And 'fore you know it—crisp brown leaves of Fall.

Subgenre

A category that is more specific than a genre that a piece of writing fits into.

Satire, allegory, parody, and pastoral are examples of **subgenres**.

Symbol

A physical object or word that represents an idea.

In many poems and plays, a red rose is a **symbol** of love.

Theme

The subject or main idea of something.

In the story of the *Turtle and the Rabbit*, the theme is that it is best to go slowly and do a good job.

Tone

The emotion that a piece of writing produces.

A letter to the mayor of your town should have a respectful, formal **tone**.

A letter to a friend might have a fun, happy **tone**.

Dear Ms. Mayor,

I am writing to tell you how happy I am that you visited our school. It was very nice to meet you.

Hey Bobby,

How are you? Things are good here. I start swim classes today. I can't wait!

Tragedy

A story that ends very badly for the main character.

Shakespeare's *Hamlet* is a **tragedy** because in the end the main character is very unhappy, and then he dies.

Body

The most important part of an essay. It is made of the middle paragraphs and tells your readers what you want them to know.

The Great Wall: A Rich History

In China, you can see a great stone dragon sliding across countryside, through mountains, and over deserts. That stone dragon is the Great Wall of China. Stretching over 4,163 miles (or 6,700 kilometers), it is the longest stone wall on the planet Earth. The Great Wall has a rich history.

The Great Wall was originally built as separate walls. These walls were meant to protect the different areas of ancient China. It is believed that the first part of the wall was built in 770 BC — that is over 2,600 years ago! Over the next 500 years, different parts of the wall were built by the states of Qin, Yan, and Zhou.

Finally, in 214 BC, Emperor Qin Shi Huang ordered that the separate walls be connected. Ten years later, the Great Wall was complete.

For centuries, the Great Wall kept China safe from invaders. Now, it is a wonder for any who have the fortune to stand and witness its winding beauty.

Brainstorm

To write down all the things you can think of on a particular topic. You can do this to get ideas for writing an essay.

Wonder of the world ← The Great Wall of China → Built many centuries ago

↓

Protected areas of China

READING STRATEGIES

LITERARY CONCEPTS

WRITING

LANGUAGE CONVENTIONS

RESEARCH

PRINTING & PUBLISHING

Bulleted list

A list that shows each item with a small dot or other shape.

Shopping list
- Water
- Fruit
- Bread

Shopping list
- ❋ Water
- ❋ Fruit
- ❋ Bread

Business letter

A letter that you write for work. Business letters have a set format.

512 Elm Street
Darwood, NY 11961
(631) 555-8290

Davis Paper Company
27 West 15th Street
Evans, MD 21105
(443) 555-1864

To Whom It May Concern,

I am sending this letter because I am a longtime customer. I felt it was important for me to let you know how much I like your quality and service.

I would recommend Davis Paper Company to anyone who needs to buy lots of paper.

Sincerely,

Moe Stiltson

Moe Stiltson

Collaborative writing

Writing with a partner or a small group.

You can get good ideas from others during **collaborative writing**.

Collect ideas

To use sources other than your own mind to find ideas on how to write about a topic.

You can read books, look at magazines, and surf the Internet to **collect ideas** for your writing.

Conclusion

The last paragraph of an essay. This is where you state your main idea for the last time.

The Great Wall: A Rich History

In China, you can see a great stone dragon sliding across countryside, through mountains, and over deserts. That stone dragon is the Great Wall of China. Stretching over 4,163 miles (or 6,700 kilometers), it is the longest stone wall on the planet Earth. The Great Wall has a rich history.

The Great Wall was originally built as separate walls. These walls were meant to protect the different areas of ancient China. It is believed that the first part of the wall was built in 770 BC — that is over 2,600 years ago! Over the next 500 years, different parts of the wall were built by the states of Qin, Yan, and Zhou.

Finally, in 214 BC, Emperor Qin Shi Huang ordered that the separate walls be connected. Ten years later, the Great Wall was complete.

For centuries, the Great Wall kept China safe from invaders. Now, it is a wonder for any who have the fortune to stand and witness its winding beauty.

Describe

To write in a way that shows what something is like.

In fall, the leaves on the ground bake slowly into reds and oranges. A crisp smell rides on the breeze.

This writing uses words that **describe** fall, like *crisp*, *red*, and *orange*. It can also be called a *description* of fall.

Writing

READING STRATEGIES

LITERARY CONCEPTS

WRITING

LANGUAGE CONVENTIONS

RESEARCH

PRINTING & PUBLISHING

Detail

A small, specific piece of information that supports a main idea or helps you see a scene in your mind.

Yesterday, I hopped on my bike, rode past Ms. Jones' Bakery, and stopped right outside my school.

Details:
hopped on my bike
rode past the bakery
stopped outside of school

Draft

One version of your writing. Every time you make a change to your writing, you create another **draft**. It usually takes many **drafts** to get a piece of writing just right.

Before

In China, you can see a great stone draggen sliding across countryside, through mountains, and over deserts. That stone draggen is the Great Wall of China. Stretching over 4,163 miles (or 6,700 kilometers), it is the longest stone wall on the planet Earth. The Great Wall has a rich history

---

Making Revisions

dragon (spelling)
In China, you can see a great stone ~~draggen~~ sliding across countryside, through mountains, and over deserts. That stone ~~draggen~~ is the Great Wall of China. Stretching over 4,163 miles (or 6,700 kilometers), it is the longest stone wall on the planet Earth. The Great Wall has a rich history. *add a period.*

New Draft

In China, you can see a great stone dragon sliding across countryside, through mountains, and over deserts. That stone dragon is the Great Wall of China. Stretching over 4,163 miles (or 6,700 kilometers), it is the longest stone wall on the planet Earth. The Great Wall has a rich history.

Edit

To improve your writing by changing words, writing better sentences, taking out confusing sentences, and moving things around that you have written.

Every time you **edit**, you make another draft.

Editorial

An essay that is mostly opinion.

Editorials are often written by the editor of a newspaper or magazine.

Elaborate

To give more information about a topic or to expand on a topic.

Chazz **elaborated** on his feelings about the book. He said it was an exciting and fun read.

Entertain

To write or say something that amuses or interests people.

Most TV shows are made to **entertain**.

Writing

READING STRATEGIES

LITERARY CONCEPTS

WRITING

LANGUAGE CONVENTIONS

RESEARCH

PRINTING & PUBLISHING

Essay

A piece of writing that gives details about one topic. An **essay** is usually short and contains facts.

The Great Wall: A Rich History

In China, you can see a great stone dragon sliding across countryside, through mountains, and over deserts. That stone dragon is the Great Wall of China. Stretching over 4,163 miles (or 6,700 kilometers), it is the longest stone wall on the planet Earth. The Great Wall has a rich history.

The Great Wall was originally built as separate walls. These walls were meant to protect the different areas of ancient China. It is believed that the first part of the wall was built in 770 BC — that is over 2,600 years ago! Over the next 500 years, different parts of the wall were built by the states of Qin, Yan, and Zhou.

Finally, in 214 BC, Emperor Qin Shi Huang ordered that the separate walls be connected. Ten years later, the Great Wall was complete.

For centuries, the Great Wall kept China safe from invaders. Now, it is a wonder for any who have the fortune to stand and witness its winding beauty.

This is an **essay** about China's Great Wall.

Exposition

Writing that informs you of something or explains something. It does not try to convince you of anything.

Birds come in many shapes and sizes, but they all have a few things in common. All birds lay eggs, and all birds have feathers.

This passage is an example of **exposition**. It tells you about birds, but it does not give you an opinion about birds.

Fact

A true statement. A **fact** can be proven or documented.

Ice melts into water when it is heated.

This sentence states a **fact**.

Formal English

The kind of language that should be used in school essays, in business letters, and at work.

Informal English: Check out the tiger!
Formal English: Observe what the tiger is doing.

Free writing

Writing without worrying about spelling, punctuation, or form. This is a good way to get your first ideas on paper.

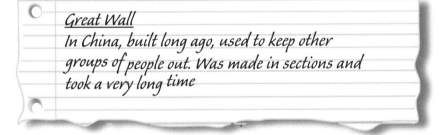

> *Great Wall*
> *In China, built long ago, used to keep other*
> *groups of people out. Was made in sections and*
> *took a very long time*

Inform

To write or say something in order to give people knowledge or facts.

A science textbook is written to **inform** you about science.

READING STRATEGIES

LITERARY CONCEPTS

WRITING

LANGUAGE CONVENTIONS

RESEARCH

PRINTING & PUBLISHING

Informal English

The kind of language you use in everyday speech and in e-mails but should not use in school writing.

Informal English: Check out the tiger!
Formal English: Observe what the tiger is doing.

Introduction

The first paragraph of an essay. This is where you tell your reader what you plan to write about.

> **The Great Wall: A Rich History**
>
> In China, you can see a great stone dragon sliding across countryside, through mountains, and over deserts. That stone dragon is the Great Wall of China. Stretching over 4,163 miles (or 6,700 kilometers), it is the longest stone wall on the planet Earth. The Great Wall has a rich history.
>
> The Great Wall was originally built as separate walls. These walls were meant to protect the different areas of ancient China. It is believed that the first part of the wall was built in 770 BC — that is over 2,600 years ago! Over the next 500 years, different parts of the wall were built by the states of Qin, Yan, and Zhou.
>
> Finally, in 214 BC, Emperor Qin Shi Huang ordered that the separate walls be connected. Ten years later, the Great Wall was complete.
>
> For centuries, the Great Wall kept China safe from invaders. Now, it is a wonder for any who have the fortune to stand and witness its winding beauty.

Journal

A book in which you can write about your feelings.

You usually do not share what you write in your **journal**.

Lead sentence

The first sentence of an essay. It is a very important sentence since it is the first thing your readers will read.

This is an example of a **lead sentence**.

> In China, you can see a great stone dragon sliding across countryside, through mountains, and over deserts.

Legible

Easy to read. Writing that is **legible** is neat and can be read without any trouble. When your handwriting is easy to read, you are writing *legibly*.

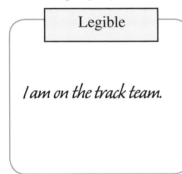

Letter

A piece of writing that is meant to go to one person. A **letter** is usually sent by mail and can be written for work or for friends.

Dear Diami,

What have you been up to lately? I tried out for the soccer team last week. I really hope I make it! What's it like in your new school?

Yours truly,
Beth

READING
STRATEGIES

LITERARY
CONCEPTS

WRITING

LANGUAGE
CONVENTIONS

RESEARCH

PRINTING
&
PUBLISHING

Main idea

The most important point in a piece of writing.

Yesterday morning, I picked up my bookbag and hopped on my bike. I zipped past Ms. Jones' Bakery, and stopped right outside my school. Ms. Bailey smiled as I took my seat in class.

Main idea: I went to school.

Memo

A short piece of writing that looks like a small letter. **Memos** have a special form, are not as formal as letters, and are usually meant to go to a small group of people.

To: Staff
From: The manager
Subject: Store closing

Our store will be closed on Saturday. We will open again on Monday morning. Have a nice weekend!

The manager

Notebook

A book where you write most of your schoolwork. You can take class notes in your **notebook**.

Opinion

A statement of what someone thinks about something. **Opinions** are not right or wrong.

Carrie's **opinion** of the movie was that it was terrible. Jane's **opinion** was that it was a great movie.

Oppose

To disagree with someone about something.

You might **oppose** going to school at night.

Organize

To keep all of your ideas, notes, and writing in order so that you will be able to find and use them later.

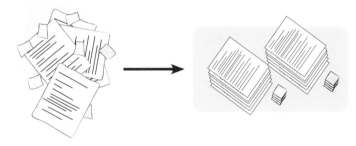

Outline

A list of all the points you want to make in the order you want to make them. It can be helpful to write an **outline** before you write an essay.

Trip Ideas:

I. Park
    a. Ride Bikes
    b. Walk
II. Beach
    a. Swim in Water
    b. Play in Sand

READING STRATEGIES

LITERARY CONCEPTS

WRITING

LANGUAGE CONVENTIONS

RESEARCH

PRINTING & PUBLISHING

READING STRATEGIES

LITERARY CONCEPTS

WRITING

LANGUAGE CONVENTIONS

RESEARCH

PRINTING & PUBLISHING

Overgeneralization

A statement that is not detailed and that assumes things that may not always be true.

All children love bears.

This sentence is an **overgeneralization** because not all children love bears. Some children do, but others may be afraid of them. Often, an **overgeneralization** will begin with the words *all* or *none*.

Paragraph

A group of sentences that focuses on one main idea. The first sentence of a **paragraph** is usually indented.

The Great Wall: A Rich History

In China, you can see a great stone dragon sliding across countryside, through mountains, and over deserts. That stone dragon is the Great Wall of China. Stretching over 4,163 miles (or 6,700 kilometers), it is the longest stone wall on the planet Earth. The Great Wall has a rich history. ◄—Paragraph 1

The Great Wall was originally built as separate walls. These walls were meant to protect the different areas of ancient China. It is believed that the first part of the wall was built in 770 BC — that is over 2,600 years ago! Over the next 500 years, different parts of the wall were built by the states of Qin, Yan, and Zhou. ◄—Paragraph 2

Finally, in 214 BC, Emperor Qin Shi Huang ordered that the separate walls be connected. Ten years later, the Great Wall was complete.

For centuries, the Great Wall kept China safe from invaders. Now, it is a wonder for any who have the fortune to stand and witness its winding beauty.

Peer review

An opinion of your writing given by someone in your class or age group. If you are asked to read and give your opinion of someone else's writing, you are giving a **peer review**.

I think Jeff's essay is good, but too long.

This is something you might say when you give a **peer review**.

Persuade

To write or speak to get someone to act or think in a specific way.

Persuasive essay

An essay that tries to make you believe something.

Lucy's **persuasive essay** got the whole community to build a park for kids.

Physical description

A description of something based on things you can see.

An apple is a red, shiny, round fruit.

READING STRATEGIES

LITERARY CONCEPTS

WRITING

LANGUAGE CONVENTIONS

RESEARCH

PRINTING & PUBLISHING

Writing

READING STRATEGIES

LITERARY CONCEPTS

WRITING

LANGUAGE CONVENTIONS

RESEARCH

PRINTING & PUBLISHING

Prewrite

To prewrite, make a list, or write a short, early version of your essay.

Benjamin Franklin's Inventions

Benjamin Franklin invented many things we still use today.

Bifocals

Lightning rod

Proofread

To check your writing to make sure that the spelling, punctuation, and sentences are correctly written.

The Great Wall: A Rich History

dragon (spelling)

In China, you can see a great stone dragon sliding across countryside, through mountains, and over deserts. That stone dragon is the Great Wall of China. Stretching over 4,163 miles (or 6,700 kilometers), it is the longest stone wall on the planet Earth. The Great Wall has a rich history. ← *add a period.*

separate (spelling)

The Great Wall was originally built as separate walls. These walls were meant to protect the different areas of ancient China. It is believed that the first part of the wall was built in 770 BC — that is over 2600 years ago! Over the next 500 years, different parts of the wall were built by the states of Qin, Yan, and Zhou.

Purpose

The reason for writing something.

The **purpose** of this book is to help you learn reading and language arts vocabulary.

READING STRATEGIES

LITERARY CONCEPTS

WRITING

LANGUAGE CONVENTIONS

RESEARCH

PRINTING & PUBLISHING

Quote

Exactly what someone has said. **Quotes** are written in quotation marks.

"What's your favorite color?" asked Kisha.
"Blue," replied Lin.

Repeat

To do or say something over and over again. Sometimes writers will **repeat** the main idea of a book so that you do not forget it. In poetry, writers may **repeat** the same words so that you hear a pattern or a beat.

In My Shoes
I took my first baby steps
in my shoes.
I went to school each day
in my shoes.
I run track races
in my shoes.
One day I'll walk for graduation
in my shoes.
Now you know
what it's like to be
in my shoes.

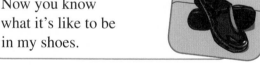

This poet **repeats** the phrase *in my shoes* throughout the poem.

Response

The things you think or the emotions you feel after you read or see something.

After I read *The Lord Of The Rings*, I felt like I had gone on a long trip with the characters. My **response** was joy that the long trip had a happy ending.

READING STRATEGIES

LITERARY CONCEPTS

WRITING

LANGUAGE CONVENTIONS

RESEARCH

PRINTING & PUBLISHING

Résumé

A specific form of writing that shows all the things you've done in school or work. If you apply for a job, you usually give a **résumé** to the person who might hire you.

Anne Gonzalez

409 West St.
(698) 555-0342
Ashton, KY 50505

Education:
High School: graduated from Deland High School in 1987
College: Two years of community college, GPA 3.26

Work Experience:
Real estate agent: Big Joe's Realty
1994—present.
Administrative assistant: Lander Community College
1990—1994.

Revise

To change your writing in any way.

Revising includes both editing and proofreading.

Salutation

The part of a letter where you greet the person you are writing to.

Dear Mr. Smith,
    I am writing to express...

Self-assessment

Looking back over your work to make a judgment about how you are doing.

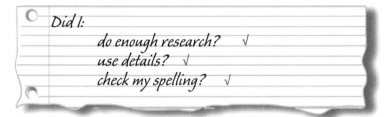

Did I:
do enough research? √
use details? √
check my spelling? √

Sensory detail

A detail that you can feel or experience by using your five senses (sight, smell, hearing, touch, and taste).

The smell of a rose is a **sensory detail**. The sharpness of a rose's thorns is another **sensory detail**.

Signature

The part of a letter where you sign your name.

Mrs. Joan Kirkland
Mrs. Joan Kirkland

Supporting sentence

A sentence that helps explain the main idea.

It is because of Franklin's great mind that we have easier lives today.

READING
STRATEGIES

LITERARY
CONCEPTS

WRITING

LANGUAGE
CONVENTIONS

RESEARCH

PRINTING
&
PUBLISHING

Thesis statement

The sentence that tells the main idea of your essay. It is different than a topic sentence, which tells the main idea of one paragraph.

This sentence is a **thesis statement**:

In my essay, I want to show that plants grow better with sunlight than they do without sunlight.

Topic

What a piece of writing is about.

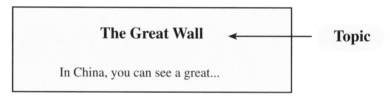

Topic sentence

The sentence in a paragraph that tells the main idea of that paragraph.

Benjamin Franklin's inventions made our lives today better.

Vague

Not clear.

Vague: Sara is okay.
Detailed: Sara is always smiling and friendly to people.

Workplace writing

Any writing you do for your job. This can include letters, memos, and résumés.

Action verb

A word that shows an action.

Zoey **kicked** the ball.
I **eat** my lunch at the table.

Active voice

A sentence written so that the subject is the noun that does the action. (Also see *passive voice*)

I threw a softball.
Dad lost his keys.

The subjects "I" and "Dad" did the actions in these **active voice** sentences.

Adjective

A word that describes a noun or pronoun.

A **tiny** bird flew between the **tall** trees.

In this sentence, the word *tiny* is an **adjective** that describes *bird*. The word *tall* is an **adjective** that describes *trees*.

Adverb

A word that describes a verb, adjective or another adverb. Many adverbs end in –ly.

A bird flew **quickly** between the trees.

In this sentence, the word *quickly* is an **adverb** that describes the word *flew*.

READING STRATEGIES

LITERARY CONCEPTS

WRITING

LANGUAGE CONVENTIONS

RESEARCH

PRINTING & PUBLISHING

Affix

A word part that attaches to the beginning or end of a word. An **affix** changes the word's meaning. Prefixes and suffixes are both **affixes**.

Color is a noun. If you add the **affix** "-ful" to it, it changes the meaning. *Colorful* is an adjective, which means *having lots of color.*

Antecedent

The word that a pronoun refers to.

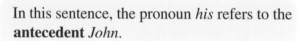

John took his dog for a walk.

In this sentence, the pronoun *his* refers to the **antecedent** *John*.

Clause

A group of words that has a subject and a verb. Every sentence has at least one **clause**, but not all **clauses** are sentences.

Papa danced.

This **clause** is a complete sentence. It has a subject (Papa) and a verb (danced). It is a complete thought.

when Papa danced

This **clause** is not a complete sentence. It has a subject (Papa) and a verb (danced). But since it also has the word *when* at the beginning, it is not a complete thought. When you read this sentence, you expect there to be more words at the end.

Collective noun

A singular noun that refers to a group of people or things as a single item.

The **class** is going on a trip.

In this sentence, *class* means a group of students.

A **flock** of birds is in that tree.

In this sentence, *flock* refers to a group of birds.

Comma splice

A writing mistake that happens when you connect two complete sentences with a comma. Instead of using a comma, you should connect two complete sentences with a conjunction (such as *for, and, nor, but, or, yet,* or *so*) or a semicolon. A **comma splice** is a type of run-on sentence.

> **Comma splice** (mistake):
> We went to the movies, we ate lots of popcorn.
>
> Correct:
> We went to the movies, **and** we ate lots of popcorn.
> We went to the movies; we ate lots of popcorn.
> We went to the movies, **where** we ate lots of popcorn.

Complement

A word that is used with a linking verb in a sentence. The linking verbs says that the subject is like something else. The **complement** tells you what the subject is like.

Marie seems **happy**.
Tad's dog is **lost**.

READING STRATEGIES

LITERARY CONCEPTS

WRITING

LANGUAGE CONVENTIONS

RESEARCH

PRINTING & PUBLISHING

Compound subject
A subject that contains more than one noun.

Grandma and Grandpa live in the city.
Gita and Stacy are going to visit them.

Compound word
A word made up of two or more other words.

paperclip (paper + clip)
handbag (hand + bag)

Conjunction
A word used to connect words, phrases, or clauses.

And, *but*, and *or* are the **conjunctions** you see most often.

A fun way to remember the most common conjunctions is to think of the word **fanboys**:
For
And
Nor
But
Or
Yet
So

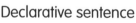

Declarative sentence
A sentence that gives information.

Canada is a country in North America.
Aunt Sara loves to go bowling.

Dependent clause

A clause that is not a complete sentence. A **dependent clause** cannot stand on its own as a sentence. (Also see *independent clause*)

now that we are here
even though she left early

Direct object

A noun or pronoun that receives the action of the verb in a sentence.

Chad threw his **coat** on the chair.

What did Chad throw? His **coat**.

He helped **her** with her homework.

Whom did he help? **Her**.

Ellipsis (…)

A punctuation mark that shows that words have been taken out of a quote or a sentence.

"A house divided…cannot stand."

The **ellipsis** tells you that there are words left out of this quote. The quote, by President Abraham Lincoln, is from a larger sentence: "A house divided *against itself* cannot stand."

READING STRATEGIES

LITERARY CONCEPTS

WRITING

LANGUAGE CONVENTIONS

RESEARCH

PRINTING & PUBLISHING

READING STRATEGIES

LITERARY CONCEPTS

WRITING

LANGUAGE CONVENTIONS

RESEARCH

PRINTING & PUBLISHING

End mark

A punctuation mark that shows when a sentence has ended. These include: the exclamation point, the period, and the question mark.

Does Ted play baseball**?**
Ted plays baseball**.**
Ted is the best**!**

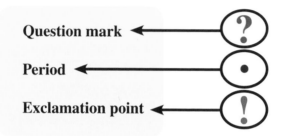

Question mark

Period

Exclamation point

Exclamatory sentence

A sentence that says something with strong feelings. This kind of sentence often ends with an *exclamation point.*

You win!
This is fun!

Fragment

A sentence that is not complete. A sentence **fragment** is usually missing either a subject or a predicate.

danced for hours and hours (no subject)
Jan, Michael, and their son (no predicate)

Future tense

A verb used to show that something will happen in the future.

We **will go** to the movies next week.
Your soup **will get** cold, so come and eat it now.

The **future tense** uses the helping verb *will.*

Gerund
A verb form ending in –ing that is used in a sentence as a noun.

Running is my favorite hobby.

In this sentence, **running** is the subject, a *thing* that someone likes to do.

Grammar
The rules that explain the way words are used in a language.

Subject-verb agreement is an example of a **grammar** rule. It lets you know the correct way to put words together.

Helping verb
A verb that helps another verb show action in a different tense.

Lee skips down the lane.
Lee **had** skipped down the lane.
Lee **will** skip down the lane.

Had and **will** help the verb *skip* in the past and future tense.

Hyphen (-)
A punctuation mark that joins words together or shows the breaks between syllables in a word. **Hyphens** are often used to connect written-out numbers or to connect some compound words.

forty-two	(connects numbers)
sister-in-law	(connects a compound word)
punc-tu-a-tion	(shows syllables)

READING STRATEGIES

LITERARY CONCEPTS

WRITING

LANGUAGE CONVENTIONS

RESEARCH

PRINTING & PUBLISHING

Imperative sentence

A sentence that tells someone to do something.

Bobby, close the door.
(you) Go to the store and buy some milk.

Often **imperative sentences** do not have a subject that is written or said aloud. In these cases, the subject is *you*.

Independent clause

A clause that can stand on its own as a complete sentence. (Also see *dependent clause*)

Dependent: when he lost the big game
Independent: He lost the big game.

Indirect object

The person or thing that receives the direct object in a sentence.

She handed **Kim** a slice of cake.

What did she hand? She handed *cake*. *Cake* is the direct object. To whom did she hand the cake? She handed cake to *Kim*. *Kim* is the **indirect object**.

Infinitive

A verb that is written without endings that show tense. The infinitive is shown by using the word "to" before the verb.

Jen likes <u>to fly</u> her kite.

      infinitive

Interjection

A word or phrase that shows emotion. Even though **interjections** are not sentences, they are usually followed by an exclamation point.

Ouch! That hurt.
You did what? **Wow!**

Ouch and *wow* are **interjections**.

Interrogative sentence

A sentence that asks for information. These sentences are also called *questions* and often end in a *question mark*.

How are you?
Has anyone seen my book?

Irregular verb

Verbs that do not follow the regular pattern when changing tense.

Regular:		**Irregular:**	
use	play	eat	write
us<u>ed</u>	play<u>ed</u>	ate	wrote

Linking verb

A verb that does not show an action. Instead, it shows how a noun or pronoun *is* or how it *seems*.

Radha **is** first in line.
The bird **seems** happy.
We **are** friends.

READING
STRATEGIES

LITERARY
CONCEPTS

WRITING

LANGUAGE
CONVENTIONS

RESEARCH

PRINTING
&
PUBLISHING

Modify

To change something or to add greater detail. Adjectives and adverbs **modify** other words.

You can **modify** the word *cat* by adding adjectives:

Striped, fluffy, orange cat.

Noun

The name of a person, place, or thing.

Kadeem brought his **books** to **school**.

In this sentence, the words *Kadeem*, *books*, and *school* are all people, places or things. They are all **nouns**.

Parts of speech

Word groups based on how each kind of word is used in writing or speaking. There are eight **parts of speech**.

Verb, Noun, Pronoun, Adjective, Adverb, Preposition, Conjunction, and Interjection

Passive voice

A sentence written so that the subject is the noun that receives the action.

Active voice: We planned the party.
Passive voice: The party was planned by us.

In the second sentence, *party* is the subject, but *us* does the planning; therefore the sentence is in the **passive voice**.

Past tense

The form of a verb that shows that the action has already happened.

My sister **worked** yesterday.

Past tense verbs often end in –ed.

Possessive

A word that tells when something belongs to a person or a thing. A **possessive** word usually ends in -**'s**.

Kelly**'s** lunch looks tasty.

Lunch belongs to Kelly.

Al borrowed Ted**'s** pencil.

Pencil belongs to Ted.

Predicate

The part of the sentence that tells what the subject is doing, plus all the words that help describe the verb.

Bernie **hit the ball with his bat**.

predicate

Prefix

A letter or group of letters added to the beginning of a word to change its meaning.

In the words *unfair*, *dislike*, and *midterm*, the **prefixes** are *un-*, *dis-*, and *mid-*.

Preposition

A word that relates one noun to another noun in a sentence. The **preposition** often tells where the noun in a sentence is located.

The library is **down** the street.
My dog sleeps **under** the table.
She brought a gift **for** me.

> **Some common prepositions are: at, by, down, for, from, in, like, near, on, of, off, out, past, through, too, up, and with.**

Prepositional phrase

A preposition along with the location the preposition refers to.

prepositional phase

The library is **down the street**.

preposition

Present tense

A verb form showing that the action in a sentence is happening right now.

Joe **rides** his bike.
I **play** outside.

Pronoun

A word that takes the place of a noun. **Pronouns** are used so that you do not have to keep repeating a noun over and over again in a sentence.

No pronouns: Carl rode Carl's bike to Carl's favorite playground.
Pronouns: Carl rode **his** bike to **his** favorite playground.

Pronouns include words like I, me, my, mine, you, your, yours, he, him, his, she, her, hers, it, its, their, theirs, and many others.

Punctuation mark

All the symbols used in writing that are not letters.

Punctuation marks include:

Question

A sentence that is used to get information. These are sometimes called *interrogative sentences*. They end in *question marks*.

Do fish get cold in winter?
When are we leaving?

Quotation marks (" ")

Punctuation marks that shows when someone is speaking. They are also used in your writing when you are repeating exactly what someone has said.

"I love apples," said Val.
Kim said that the roses were "beautiful."

READING STRATEGIES

LITERARY CONCEPTS

WRITING

LANGUAGE CONVENTIONS

RESEARCH

PRINTING & PUBLISHING

READING STRATEGIES

LITERARY CONCEPTS

WRITING

LANGUAGE CONVENTIONS

RESEARCH

PRINTING & PUBLISHING

Regular verb

A verb that changes into different tenses using regular English patterns.

pick   walk
pick**ed**   walk**ed**
will pick   **will** walk

Root

The main word to which an affix is attached.

un-**friend**-ly
over-**excite**-d

In these example, *friend* and *excite* are the **roots**.

Run-on sentence

A writing error that happens when two sentences are joined together without a conjunction or semicolon. A comma splice is a type of **run-on sentence**.

        , and
Troy was at a party ^ he had a lot of fun.

This **run-on sentence** needs a comma and the word *and* to make it correct:
Troy was at a party, and he had a lot of fun.

Sentence

A group of words containing a subject and a predicate that expresses a complete thought.

Bonnie sailed in a boat.
Did you and Amanda eat rice for lunch?

Simple predicate
The verb of the sentence.

My sister **walked** up the stairs.
Jerry **eats** ice cream.

Simple subject
The noun or pronoun that is the subject of the sentence.

My **sister** walked up the stairs.
Jerry loves ice cream.

Subject
The simple subject of a sentence along with all of its modifiers.

My tired little sister walked up the stairs.
Carmen's uncle Jerry loves ice cream.

Subject-verb agreement
A rule stating that when the subject of a sentence is singular, the verb must be singular, and when the subject of a sentence is plural, the verb must be plural.

He sits by the window.

In this sentence, the subject **He** and the verb **sits** are both singular.

We sit by the window.

In this sentence, the subject **We** and the verb **sit** are both plural.

READING STRATEGIES

LITERARY CONCEPTS

WRITING

LANGUAGE CONVENTIONS

RESEARCH

PRINTING & PUBLISHING

Suffix

A letter or group of letters added to the end of a word to change its meaning.

In the words *location*, *kingdom*, and *smiling*, the **suffixes** are –*tion*, -*dom*, and –*ing*.

Verb

A word showing an action or a state of being.

Luci **flew** in a plane today.
It **has been** cold and rainy for weeks.

Verb tense

The different ways a verb is written to show the time when something happens.

Past: Kathy **jumped** in the pool.
Present: Kathy **jumps** in the pool.
Future: Kathy **will jump** in the pool.

Catalog

A list of all the items a library has available to you. This is usually the best place to start looking for information in a library.

Clip file

A collection of news articles, magazine clippings, and pictures that you keep to give you ideas for what to write about in the future. A **clip file** can also mean a place where you keep copies of anything you write that has been published.

Database

A large collection of information that you can use to find out facts.

Some **databases**, such as science research **databases**, are for one subject only. Others have a wide range of types of information.

Dictionary

A book that alphabetically lists many words along with their meanings, parts of speech, and instructions on how to say the word.

Patt-ern: *noun.* (pronunciation: PAT-urn) 1. Something that is repeated over and over again. 2. Something used as a model for making things.

Encyclopedia

A book or set of books that gives lots of information on many different subjects, usually in volumes according to the letters of the alphabet. Some **encyclopedias** are online or on CDs.

Fact-check

To make sure that something you say or write is correct by looking it up in other sources.

Daniel **fact-checked** his report on dairy farming by looking up information about dairy farming in an encyclopedia.

Internet

The network of computers all over the world that allows you to find information on just about any topic. The **Internet** gives us access to e-mail, many databases, and other resources.

Many people use and put information on the **Internet**. Some information is fact while other information is opinion.

Research

To look for facts and information on a particular subject.

I did **research** on comets by looking up the word *comet* on the Internet.

Source

A place where you find information. **Sources** can be databases, encyclopedias, and the Internet; but they can also be lines from poetry, novels, or short stories.

In Rafael's report about 19th century novels, his first **source** was *The Red Badge of Courage*.

Statistic

Numerical information.

There are over 200,000 miles of coastline on Earth.

This sentence is a **statistic** about the Earth.

Survey

A list of questions that ask the opinions of many people. The answers to the questions are then used to show how large groups of people feel about a topic.

In a **survey** of favorite school subjects, 3 out of every 10 students say that reading is their favorite.

Survey

Favorite school subject _____

Favorite sports team _____

Favorite kind of food _____

READING STRATEGIES

LITERARY CONCEPTS

WRITING

LANGUAGE CONVENTIONS

RESEARCH

PRINTING & PUBLISHING

61

Thesaurus

A book that lists words along with their synonyms and antonyms.

happy *adjective* Having pleasure or showing pleasure; Synonyms: content, glad, joyful (Antonym: sad)

Works cited list

A list of sources you have used for information in your own work. A works cited list is sometimes called a *bibliography*.

Works Cited List

Brown, Raymond. "My Place In The Sun." *My City Paper*. 13 July 2008. http://www.mycitypaper.com/news/story

Twain, Mark. *The Adventures of Tom Sawyer (Revised Edition)*. California:. University of California Press, 2002.

Document
Any piece of writing.

Letters, flyers, and brochures are all types of **documents**.

Flyer
A one-page document that can be copied and handed out to many people. **Flyers** usually give information about events or meetings.

PLANT
SALE
Monday the 12th from:
8:00 a.m.-3:00 p.m.

3088 Only Rd,
Princess Anne, MD
21030

Font
The style and size of the letters you use in a document. There are thousands of **fonts**, and each one will make your writing look and feel different.

There are many different fonts.
Look for one you like.
Make sure it is easy to read!

Formatting

Placing your words in a document in a specific way. The reason a letter looks different from an essay is because each one uses a different **format**.

Letter Format

512 Elm Street
Darwood, NY 11961
(631) 555-8290

Davis Paper Company
27 West 15th Street
Evans, MD 21105
(443) 555-1864

To Whom It May Concern,

I am sending this letter because I am a longtime customer. I felt it was important for me to let you know how much I like your quality and service.

I would recommend Davis Paper Company to anyone who needs to buy lots of paper.

Sincerely,

Moe Stiltson

Essay Format

The Great Wall: A Rich History

In China, you can see a great stone dragon sliding across countryside, through mountains, and over deserts. That stone dragon is the Great Wall of China. Stretching over 4,163 miles (or 6,700 kilometers), it is the longest stone wall on the planet Earth. The Great Wall has a rich history.

The Great Wall was originally built as separate walls. These walls were meant to protect the different areas of ancient China. It is believed that the first part of the wall was built in 770 BC — that is over 2,600 years ago! Over the next 500 years, different parts of the wall were built by the states of Qin, Yan, and Zhou.

Finally, in 214 BC, Emperor Qin Shi Huang ordered that the separate walls be connected. Ten years later, the Great Wall was complete.

For centuries, the Great Wall kept China safe from invaders. Now, it is a wonder for any who have the fortune to stand and witness its winding beauty.

Journal

A magazine that prints writing by experts in a field of study.

Medical doctors can use the *Journal of the American Medical Association* to learn about new discoveries in medicine.

Literary magazine

A magazine that prints creative writing. Some **literary magazines** print all types of writing. Others print only one kind of writing, such as poetry or short stories.

Printing & Publishing

Page layout

Placing words, images and pictures on a document page.

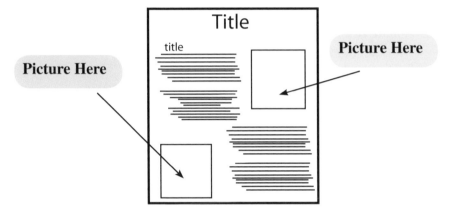

Pamphlet

A document printed on one piece of paper and then folded. **Pamphlets** are often used as advertisements.

Periodical

Any publication that is printed on a regular basis.

The daily newspaper is a **periodical**; a monthly magazine is a **periodical**, too.

READING STRATEGIES

LITERARY CONCEPTS

WRITING

LANGUAGE CONVENTIONS

RESEARCH

PRINTING & PUBLISHING

READING STRATEGIES

LITERARY CONCEPTS

WRITING

LANGUAGE CONVENTIONS

RESEARCH

PRINTING & PUBLISHING

Portfolio

A collection of all the best writing or artwork you have created.

A poet's **portfolio** will be full of poems. An artist's **portfolio** may contain drawings, photographs, or even paintings.

Publication

Any written form of media printed for a large audience.

Publications include newspapers, magazines, books, journals, pamphlets, and many other forms of media.

Publish

To print words, music, or images on paper either to hand out or to sell. **Publishing** can also include putting work on the internet for people to read.

Index

Index

Credits ✳

Many thanks to the following organizations for the use of their photography and/or illustrations in this publication:

Integration and Application Network, University of Maryland Center for Environmental Science, ian.umces.edu/symbols

National Oceanic and Atmospheric Administration www.noaa.gov

USDA Agricultural Research Service www.nass.usda.gov

US Fish and Wildlife Service www.fws.gov

Additional Photo Credits
Capstone Press, cover, i (bounce illustration, image of man)
Ingram Publishing, cover, i (comedy/tragedy masks)
Shutterstock/Lukasz Kwapien, cover, i (book open to pages)

Notes